# DREAM
# BIG

T0004389

# SIMPLE SUCCESS GUIDES

*How to Live on 24 Hours a Day*
*The Game of Life and How to Play It*
*The Go-Getter*
*The Golden Key*

# DREAM BIG

## Overcoming Fear and Achieving Success

## NAPOLEON HILL

ST. MARTIN'S
**ESSENTIALS**
**NEW YORK**

The information in this book is not intended to replace the advice of the reader's own physician or other medical professional. You should consult a medical professional in matters relating to health, especially if you have existing medical conditions, and before starting, stopping, or changing the dose of any medication you are taking. Individual readers are solely responsible for their own health-care decisions. The author and the publisher do not accept responsibility for any adverse effects individuals may claim to experience, whether directly or indirectly, from the information contained in this book.

Published in the United States by St. Martin's Essentials, an imprint of St. Martin's Publishing Group.

INTRODUCTION. Copyright © 2022 by Joel Fotinos. All rights reserved. Printed in the United States of America. For information, address St. Martin's Publishing Group, 120 Broadway, New York, NY 10271.

www.stmartins.com

The Library of Congress Cataloging-in-Publication Data is available upon request.

ISBN 978-1-250-86186-3 (trade paperback)
ISBN 978-1-250-86188-7 (ebook)

"Adversity—A Blessing in Disguise" was first published in 1915.
"Let Ambition Be Your Master" was first published in 1917.
"What I Have Learned from Analyzing Ten Thousand People" was first published in 1917.
"Self Control" was first published in 1920.
"A Definite Aim in Life" was first published in 1920.
*The Law of Success* was first published in 1925.
*Think and Grow Rich* was first published in 1937.

Our books may be purchased in bulk for promotional, educational, or business use. Please contact your local bookseller or the Macmillan Corporate and Premium Sales Department at 1-800-221-7945, extension 5442, or by email at MacmillanSpecialMarkets@macmillan.com.

First St. Martin's Essentials Edition: 2022

This edition seeks to faithfully reproduce the original publications of the author's works, and so has maintained the original spelling and grammar throughout, with only minor alterations for clarity or content.

10  9  8  7  6  5  4  3  2  1

# CONTENTS

# INTRODUCTION

By Joel Fotinos

This little volume contains gigantic ideas. If you have dreams, then the ideas contained within can help!

Let's start with a little background information. *Dream Big* is a selection of some of Napoleon Hill's most inspirational and motivational writings on the topic of living your dreams. Hill is most known for his bestselling book *Think and Grow Rich*, which has sold millions of copies since its initial publication in 1937, and continues to inspire millions of readers every year. Hill also helmed several magazines (from which some of the writings in this volume originated), as well as several more books. It has been said that Hill inspired more people to become millionaires and billionaires than any other writer in modern history.

Five of the little chapters in this book are from articles that Hill wrote approximately a hundred years ago. Three of the chapters are adapted from Hill's magnus opus *Think and Grow Rich,* and the final chapter is material taken from his encyclopedic book

*The Law of Success*. But all of it is aimed to show the reader—you!—that there are definite steps to take in the attainment of passions and goals. Perhaps it will inspire you to go and read Hill's other writings.

It's important to note that while the ideas Hill writes about are timeless, Hill's writing was very much of his time. His work is easy to read, but at times the examples he uses, or the language he uses, will seem old-fashioned. This is especially true in his use of the masculine pronoun, and using the word "man" to describe "humankind," which was the norm of his time. We've left this intact, in the effort to keep this material as accurate to his original writings as possible.

But *Dream Big* isn't about Napoleon Hill, it's about YOU. The ideas in this volume were chosen to give practical, time-honored advice on such important topics as finding your definite aim in life, turning failure and adversity into blessings, protecting yourself from negative influences, overcoming our own self-defeating attitudes (he calls them "alibis"), and overcoming fear.

There are longer books by Napoleon Hill than *Dream Big*, but there aren't any that have more heart! I invite you to read this book like a short guide to empowerment, with advice by a life coach who wants to help you succeed. Read each little chapter, and then ask yourself which ideas most resonate with you, and perhaps write those down in the margin or in a journal. Next, ask what actions the chapter asks or inspires you to take, and write those down as well. And then . . . take those actions!

Great success is built step by step. Let this book help you find some steps to take toward your success.

One more thing . . .

Enjoy the journey. This book has several reminders that we aren't meant to live small, scared lives. We are meant, Hill would tell us, to have a passion (definite aim) that burns a powerful flame in our hearts. That fire fuels us to wake each day with enthusiasm and make as many positive choices toward that goal as we can. We can overcome our fears, our alibis, and our procrastination.

How? Turn the page . . .

# ADVERSITY—
# A BLESSING IN
# DISGUISE

Friend, do not become discouraged, disappointed and disheartened, if the seemingly cruel hand of fate knocks you off of your feet. Maybe the blow will prove to be the greatest blessing that ever came your way.

It has happened to many and doubtless it will happen to you, when the dark clouds of despair have darkened the pathway of life's progress, that behind each dark cloud is a silver lining, if we only learn how to see it.

There were two men who established and built up an enormously successful commercial institution. They owned the stock in the company about equally. One of the men, who had lots of initiative, began selling off some of his stock, thus enjoying for personal use a large amount of ready cash from the proceeds.

His associate in the business, who didn't possess quite so much initiative, wanted to sell some of his personal stock that he might also enjoy some ready cash from the proceeds. But not a dollar could he sell. He appealed to his associate who was finding a ready market for his stock, requesting the associate to help him dispose of his stock. But the associate refused, suggesting that "he do his own selling." This refusal resulted in a serious disagreement between the two men, which finally ended in a complete dissolution of their friendly business relations.

Now let us see what happens. The one who could not find a market for his stock was the fortunate one in the final crisis. The one with the ready initiative, who sold his stock, sold with it by so doing, his voice in the management of the business. When the climax was reached in their disagreement, the one who couldn't sell his stock naturally had, BY FORCE OF CIRCUM-STANCES, the control of the business, so he used his power to his own salvation and to the great detriment of his associate, by voting him out of the Presidency of the corporation and voting himself into that office.

The fact that he couldn't sell his stock was A BLESSING IN DISGUISE.

There was once a young man who was President of a corporation which was making lots of money. He owned automobiles, had servants and all the other luxuries which go with a successful business. He trusted his banker too far by borrowing money for expansion purposes. The banker wanted this young man's interest in the corporation, because he knew the young man was making lots of money and the banker happened to be dishonest. In the 1907 Roosevelt Panic he saw his chance and closed him out. It seemed like a dark day for the young man. All was lost. But watch the roulette wheel of destiny as it spins around by the force of the hand of fate. His loss forced him to go back to the practice of law. This brought him in touch with a million-dollar corporation which employed him at a salary of $5,000.00 a year, a salary which he wouldn't have thought of accepting from an outsider while he was in control of his own business. This brought him to the middle west, and likewise in touch with the "big opportunity" of his life.

So his loss proved a blessing in disguise, for it literally drove him into a greater success.

A young bank clerk was discharged on account of his habit of drawing pictures of automobiles and sketching mechanical parts of automobiles during business hours. The loss of his job was quite a shock to him, for he supported his mother and two sisters from his small earnings as a bank clerk.

The loss of his bank job was the greatest blessing that ever came to him, for six months later he invented an automobile part which made him a fortune. He is now president of the largest automobile accessories companies in America. His clerks are all supplied with desk pads and pencils, with instructions to do all the drawing of automobiles they wish, and to submit to him any new ideas for improvements of automobile parts. Any of their ideas which he uses are paid for extra, at one hundred dollars each.

John D. Rockefeller discharged one of his faithful employees who he thought went too far in the exercise of his authorized duties, in making a financial transaction for Mr. Rockefeller in his absence, even though the deal netted Mr. Rockefeller several thousand dollars in cash.

A blessing in disguise. This office clerk, who had been honest and faithful, but not overly well paid, was immediately employed by one of Mr. Rockefeller's rivals, at a handsome salary. He now holds a high official position with the rival company.

And, while I write, further evidence of the soundness of my theory that "Adversity is usually a blessing in disguise" reaches me. One of the men mentioned in the beginning of this narrative—the one who was successful in selling stock, but who thereby lost the presidency of his company—has been elected president of a ten-million-dollar corporation, with an excellent chance to make $50,000.00 a year from his salary and dividends on his bonus stock in the company.

The ten-million-dollar corporation never would have been organized in all probability, except for the fact that this man's business associate supplanted him in his original position.

A blessing in disguise, for the ten-million-dollar corporation has patents and secret processes for making fuel, heat and light which probably will make this man immensely wealthy.

Every change in one's environment is for a purpose. That which seems like disappointment and ill "luck" usually is a blessing in disguise. If we do not carefully study cause and effect in all that we do and all that comes our way, we may never discover when and where our apparent failures are, in reality, blessings instead.

Stop and take an inventory of your life's record and see if you cannot find evidence in your own case which will support the correctness of this. Take an inventory of the lives of those you know intimately and see if the same is not true.

Then, when you become discouraged; when the hand of fate seems to be against you; when your destiny seems doubtful and life's pathway fraught with many thorns of disappointment; when the rough and rugged hand of time spins the roulette wheel of fate so hard that the little pointer goes past your number just remember, friends, that there is a bigger stake awaiting you, if not in your present environment, then later on in some other "game" in the sphere of human accomplishments.

Hang on!

# LET AMBITION BE
# YOUR MASTER

LUCKY is the man who is driven by that determined little slave master called AMBITION! Those who have enjoyed the greatest success in life were literally driven to succeed by AMBITION! It made Harriman, Rockefeller, Carnegie, Hill, Roosevelt, and a good many thousands of other successful men of whom we never hear.

Ambition is the mainspring of life, but we must keep it wound up! Self-confidence is the balance wheel which keeps ambition moving at an even momentum. Enthusiasm is the oil with which we keep the human machine greased and in smooth running order. The well-organized, capable, and productive man is AMBITIOUS, ENTHUSIASTIC, and, possesses plenty of SELF-CONFIDENCE. Without these success is uncertain, if not impossible.

One of the greatest men America has ever known divorced his first wife because she was beneath his mental plane, and therefore had a tendency to keep down his ambition. This great man is not with us any more, but the world is testifying to his greatness by quoting his writings and reading his books more than ever before. It is a commonly known fact that his second wife was his chief source of inspiration—that she was responsible for keeping his AMBITION alive and constantly on the alert. That is why he married her. He foresaw the need for a constant attendant who would see to it that his AMBITION let him have no rest.

Lucky is the man who has formed a partnership with such a wife. We all get lazy at times. We need someone to keep our AMBITION alive and spur us on to bigger and better accomplishment. The chief reason that I consent to my wife going back to the farm every summer is that while she is away she constantly writes me letters which fire me with AMBITION. She understands me as few wives understand their husbands. She knows how necessary it is to constantly remind me of my *chief aims in life*, and she has a way of doing it which is pleasing and inspiring.

When I secured my first $5,000 a year position I thought I was fixed for life, and probably I would have been, had it not been for that little master for whom I was slaving—AMBITION! My wife and AMBITION collaborated against me and made me resign that position—FOR A BIGGER ONE! Five thousand a year would have satisfied me had it not been for my master, AMBITION. In my bigger and broader field I serve a hundred of my fellow men where I served one before, which means that I get a hundred times as much enjoyment out of life as well as financial returns which are adequate and in proportion to the service which I perform.

In addition to my regular work I lecture three times a week in one of the local colleges, on the subject of Advertising and Salesmanship. The course is a heavy one, covering a period of ten months. The students are taught everything about Advertising and Selling that I can teach them, both from my own experience and from that of a score or more of able advertising specialists. THE FIRST LECTURE IN THE COURSE IS ON THE SUBJECT OF THE VALUE OF AMBITION! I use every ounce of influence that I possess to fire these young men and young women with an everlasting knowledge of the value of AMBITION, SELF-CONFIDENCE, and ENTHUSIASM! If I succeed no further than to cause my students to cultivate that wonderful power, AMBITION, my time and theirs will have been well spent in the effort.

AMBITION is what freed America from over-the-sea rulership.

Once in my life, while I was working for a salary, I was discharged from my position—just ONCE! The head of the institution for which I worked told me that I was too "ambitious." That was the greatest compliment anyone ever paid me, even though it cut me off temporarily from my bread and meat.

I have always had my suspicions why this man "fired" me, although he claimed it was because his "help" were unanimously agreed that I ought to go! His "help" who objected to me was one of his brothers who had his eye on the General Managership of the institution. He knew what "AMBITION" might lead me to. I have never blamed the brother, for he has a wife and two babies to support, and "AMBITION" on my part seemed to him a dangerous barrier between him and his coveted goal.

That institution of which I write was organized nearly twenty years ago. It is doing a business of about $600,000 a year. Another institution, engaged in the same line of business, started in just six years ago, on a capital of less than $6,000. I was formerly Advertising Manager of this institution. It does not discourage "AMBITION." It is now doing a business of $1,500,000 a year, and clearing more net profits every month than the other firm is doing in gross business. The older institution, the one which was organized and has been doing business for nearly twenty years, is headed by men who are afraid of the "AMBITIOUS MAN." Those who are working for a salary are afraid he will get their jobs (which said fear is not without some foundation). The head of the firm is afraid of the "AMBITIOUS MAN" because he is afraid he will find in him a compeitor in business (which, also, is not without well-grounded foundation).

BUT—AND HERE IS THE CRUX OF MY WHOLE STORY OF THESE TWO FIRMS— THE MAJORITY OF BUSINESS FIRMS ARE LOOKING FOR MEN WHO HAVE PLENTY OF "AMBITION." Do not worry because one firm is afraid of the ambitious man. The very fact that such a firm is afraid of him is, in itself, strong evidence of weakness on the part of those who manage the firm.

While I was Advertising Manager of the younger firm of which I have written, I had three young men in my department. I put them on notice that some day one of them would get my position, and I commenced training them for my job. I told them that the man who "made good" first would get the place, if my recommendations would help any. My Secretary landed the prize. He is still with that firm, making more money than he ever made in his life, and more money than the average man of his age receives. I did not discourage "AMBITION" for fear of losing my job. I encouraged it so that someone would grow to be big enough to push me out of the rut and into a bigger position. That is what happened. I have no patience to speak of, with the man who is so narrow that he is afraid to inspire "AMBITION" in his fellow workers.

Show me a man who believes he has a corner on the details connected with his job and I will show you, in the same person, a man who will never develop beyond petty selfishness. I beseech you not to fall into the habit of neglecting to cultivate your "AMBITION." You will need something more than mere services with which to succeed. You will need that ever alert little master which is the subject of this chapter. But, I must here give you a word of warning—*do not let your ambition become a selfish one!* The greatest object over which to develop ambition is the desire to serve our fellow men. We cannot serve them if we are jealous of them. Remember, also, that AMBITION is a contagious thing. If you give it to the world, the world will give it back to you in increased measure. But keep it unto yourself and you will lose it. It will take wings and fly!

Ambition finds expression in a thousand different forms. It is the foundation which underlies all invention, art, music, industry, commerce—nay, the very foundation upon which the progress of the world has been built. Within the present generation we have seen it expressed in the most wonderful inventions the world has ever known; the automobile, the telephone, the wireless, the submarines, the X-ray, and the airplane. AMBITION was the very warp and woof out of which these things were constructed. Ambition leads us to think, and when we begin to think the nebulous problems in the world's evolution begin to become clarified and simplified. BE AMBITIOUS IF NOTHING MORE. OTHER THINGS WILL TAKE CARE OF THEMSELVES.

# WHAT I HAVE LEARNED FROM ANALYZING TEN THOUSAND PEOPLE

WHEN I was requested to write this article, I was overjoyed at such an opportunity to pass on to thoughtful men and women, who are trying to "find themselves," the benefit of my experience as a personal analyst.

During the past eight years I have analyzed over ten thousand men and women who were earnestly seeking their proper niche in the world's work. Incidentally, through my research I have discovered some of the fundamental qualities without which no human being can hope for success. Five of these are mentioned in this article, in words which a school boy can easily understand.

I have also discovered some of the things which break men's hearts and send them to the scrap-heap of human failures. It is my sincere hope that every person who reads this article may profit by one or more of the points which it covers. I am placing the results of my discoveries in print for the first time, solely out of my deep desire to make life's pathway just a little smoother for my fellow man.

It is my purpose to pass on to you, in as few words as possible, that portion of my discoveries which I believe will aid you in planning and achieving your "chief aim" in life, whatever that may be. I shall not preach to you. Whatever suggestions I make are based upon discoveries which I have made in my work.

I believe it befitting to state that twenty years ago I was working as a laborer, at wages of $1 a day. I had no home and no friends. I had but little education. My future then looked very unpromising. I was downcast in spirit. I had no ambition. I had no definite purpose in life. All around me I saw men, some young and some old, who were whipped—just as I felt that I was. I absorbed my environment as a sponge absorbs water. I became a part of the daily routine in which I lived.

It had never occurred to me that I could ever amount to anything. I believed my lot in life was to be that of a laborer. I was just like a horse which has had the bit slipped into its mouth and the saddle buckled on its back.

Here is the turning point in my career. Note it well!

A chance remark, no doubt made in a half-jocular way, caused me to throw the bit out of my mouth, kick off the saddle, and "run away" as young horses sometimes do. That remark was made by a farmer with whom I lived. I shall never forget it if I live to be a hundred, because it has partly bridged the gap over that awful chasm which nearly all human beings want to cross, "failure"!

The remark was this: "You are a bright boy. What a pity you are not in school instead of at work as a laborer at a dollar a day."

"You are a bright boy!" These were the sweetest words I had ever heard.

That remark aroused in me the first ambition I had ever felt, and, incidentally, it is directly responsible for the personal analysis system which I have worked out. No one had ever hinted to me before that I was "bright." I had always imagined that I was exceedingly dull. In fact, I had been told that I was a dunce. As a boy I was defeated in everything I undertook, largely because those with whom I associated ridiculed me and discouraged me from engaging in the things which interested me most. My work was selected for me—my associates were selected for me—my studies were selected for me—and my play, well, I was taught that play was a waste of time.

With this first-hand knowledge of the great handicap under which the average person starts out in life, as a working basis, I began many years ago to work out a system for helping people "find themselves" as early in life as possible. My efforts have yielded splendid returns for I have helped many find the work for which they were most suited, and started them on the road to happiness and success. I have helped not a few to acquire the qualities for success which are mentioned in this article.

## THE FIRST TWO SUCCESS REQUISITES

With this prelude I shall tell you first what I believe to be the two most important of the five chief requisites for success. These are SELF-CONFIDENCE and ENTHUSIASM. The other three I will mention later.

What is self-confidence?

I will tell you what it is: It is the little glass window through which you may look and see the real man-power within your body. Self-confidence is self-discovery—finding out who you are and what you can do. It is the banishment of fear. It is the acquirement of mental courage. It is the turning on of the light of human intelligence, through the use of common sense.

It was self-confidence, plus enthusiasm and concentration, that caused the birth of the world's greatest inventions, the incandescent electric light, the automobile, the talking machine, the airplane, the moving picture, and all the other great mechanical creations.

Self-confidence, then, is an essential quality for all worth-while accomplishments. Yet, it is the quality in which most of us are weakest. Not a weakness which many of us acknowledge, but it exists just the same. A man without self-confidence is like a ship without a rudder—he wastes his energy without moving in the right direction.

I wish I might be able to tell you exactly how to acquire full self-confidence. That would be a big undertaking. I will give you this suggestion, however—I made my first step in the direction of self-confidence the day I heard those words, "You are a bright boy." That was the first time I had ever felt ambition tugging at my coat sleeve, and with it, apparently, came self-confidence.

It is remarkable what clothes have to do with building self-confidence. A man came to me for analysis not long ago. He had been earning a good salary, but conditions for which he was in no way responsible caused him to be let out. I asked him how much money he had and he said, "Seventy-five dollars." I told him to invest one-third of it in a new suit of clothes. He demurred on the ground that he "couldn't afford it." But I insisted and went with him to buy the clothes. Then I insisted on his going to the cobbler's and having the heels of his shoes straightened up. Then I persuaded him to have his shoes shined and get a clean shave and a hair cut. I then sent him to see the president of a large corporation who employed him at $3,000 a year.

If I had sent him to interview the president of that corporation without the new suit and the clean-up, he wouldn't have gotten the position, in all probability, because he would not have had the proper self-confidence. Good clothes, clean linen, polished shoes, and a clean shave are not luxuries—they are a necessity to the man who comes in contact with the business public.

## THE SECOND SUCCESS REQUISITE

Then comes the second requisite for success, enthusiasm, that great dynamic force which puts self-confidence into action. Enthusiasm may be likened to the steam which runs the locomotive. The most powerful locomotive ever built might stand upon the side-track with coal in the bunker and the engineer in the cab, but if there is no steam, the wheels will not turn—there is no action.

It is exactly the same with the human machine. If there is no enthusiasm, there is little or no action. Lack of these qualities—self-confidence and enthusiasm—stands between the great majority of men and success. This statement is no mere conjecture upon my part. I have proved it in thousands of cases. I am proving it in more than a hundred cases a week right along. Enthusiasm is something which cannot be counterfeited. Only the real article will fill the bill. Enthusiasm usually comes automatically when you find the vocation into which you can pitch your whole heart and soul—the work you love best.

## THE THIRD SUCCESS REQUISITE

The third requisite for success is a definite working plan—the habit of working with a "chief aim" in life. From my work as a vocational director, I have learned that most people have no such plan. Men who are working without a well-defined plan—without a predetermined objective—are going no-where in particular and most of them are getting nowhere. In my personal Analysis Chart, which all whom I examine must fill out, is this question.

"What is your 'chief aim' in life?"

An actual tabulation of answers to this question shows that only one out of every fifty has any "chief aim." But few have any sort of a real aim, "chief" or otherwise. Yet, nearly all whom I have analyzed expect to succeed. Just when or how or in what work the majority of them do not undertake to say.

Nearly every man wants a "big position," yet not one

out of a hundred, even though he may be competent, knows how to get it. A "big position" is not something that we find hanging on a bush ready to be plucked off by "pull" by the first person who comes along. It is the sum total of a number of smaller positions or tasks which we have efficiently filled; not necessarily with different firms, but, as often as otherwise, in the employment of one firm. A big position is built just as we build a big skyscraper—by first formulating a definite plan and then building according to that plan, step by step.

The possible exception to this rule is the man who gets into a "big position" through "pull." There are exceptions to most rules, but the question to ask yourself is this: "Am I willing to go through life and take a chance on getting ahead on 'pull'?" Look about you and I dare say you will find that for every man who is succeeding by "pull" you may find a hundred who are succeeding by "push"!

There are varying degrees of success, just as there are different ideas as to what success is, but whether your idea of success is the accumulation of wealth or the rendering of some great service to mankind, or both, you will not likely achieve it unless you have a "chief aim"—a definite goal with a definite plan mapped out for reaching it.

No architect ever started a building until he had first created a perfect picture of it in his mind, and then carefully transferred the detail of the picture to a blueprint. And no human being may hope to build a worthwhile success until he has planned the building and decided what it shall be.

## SELECTING A VOCATION

A very large proportion of the people whom I have analyzed are in positions which they hold, not by **selection,** but by **chance.** Even those who are following vocations which they deliberately chose, in the majority of cases, have not observed even the most elementary rules of self-analysis. They have never stopped to find out whether or not the work in which they are engaged is the work for which they are best fitted by nature and education.

For example, a young man whom I recently analyzed, had prepared himself for the practice of law, but had made an utter failure of that profession. He failed, first, because he did not like the profession after he got into it; secondly, because he had absolutely no native ability for that profession. He was badly deformed physically and, as a consequence, made a very poor impression before courts and juries. He lacked enthusiasm and that dynamic force which we call "personality," without which he could not hope to succeed as a lawyer. Such a person might succeed to some extent as advisory counsel or "office lawyer," but not as a trial lawyer where a strong personality and the ability to speak with force and conviction count for so much.

The surprising part of this particular case was the fact that this man had never understood just why he did not succeed in the practice of law. It seemed simple enough to him after I had pointed out the negative qualities which I believed had stood between him and success. When I asked him how he came to take up law, he replied, "Well, I just had a hunch that I would like it!"

"I just had a hunch that I would like it!"

Selecting a life work on a "hunch" is a dangerous thing. You wouldn't purchase a race-horse on a "hunch"; you would want to see him perform on the track. You wouldn't purchase a bird-dog on a "hunch"; you would want to see him in action or know something of his pedigree. If you selected a bird-dog in this haphazard way, you might find yourself trying to set birds with a bull-pup!

A court reporter, whom I analyzed, said to me: "My fifteen years of experience have proved to me that a jury seldom tries the defendant, but instead, they try the lawyers in the case. The lawyer who makes the best impression generally wins." Everyone who is familiar with court actions knows that this is too often true. You can see, therefore, what an important part "personality" plays in the practice of law.

Mr. Carnegie says that his success is due largely to his ability to pick men. Mr. Frank A. Vanderlip and Mr. Rockefeller say the same. If you will stop and analyze all the successful men you know, you will probably find that they either possess all the requisites for success in the business in which they are engaged, or, they know how to select men who will supply what they lack— men who are their opposites in nearly every particular.

Probably 50% of those who call themselves salesmen are of poor personal appearance, have weak faces, and speak without force. A salesman conveys to his prospective buyer a positive or negative influence, according to his own personality and manner of approach in presenting his case. A man who is badly deformed, or the man who suffers from impediment of speech and otherwise makes a negative appearance had better not take up oral salesmanship. If he can hide behind the written page, he may succeed, but in person never!

## THE FOURTH SUCCESS REQUISITE

The fourth success requisite is the habit of performing more service than you are actually paid for. It is the practice of the majority of men to perform no more service than they feel they are being paid to perform. Fully 80% of all whom I have analyzed were suffering on account of this great mistake.

You need have no fear of competition from the man who says, "I'm not paid to do that, therefore I'll not do it." He will never be a dangerous competitor for your job, but watch out for the fellow who does not let his pick hang in the air when the whistle blows, or the man who stays at his desk or work bench until his work is finished—watch out that such a fellow does not "Challenge you at the post and pass you at the grandstand," as Andrew Carnegie said.

Before mentioning the fifth and last requisite for success I shall ask your indulgence while I digress for just a few moments. After I had commenced work on this article I decided to have the five points which I have covered put to the acid test to see whether or not they would square up with the experience of other vocational directors. I took the manuscript to Dr. J. M. Fitzgerald, Chicago, who is, without doubt, the most able vocational director in the world.

Dr. Fitzgerald went over the manuscript with me word for word and I have his permission to quote him as saying that he fully endorses the five chief points covered by this article. He says that they square up with his own experience, exactly. But, before we went over the manuscript, I asked Dr. Fitzgerald to state the chief negative qualities which he had discovered to be

standing as barriers between those whom he had analyzed and success. His reply was quick and concise, as
follows:

1. Lack of self-discernment; the lack of ability
   upon part of most men to analyze themselves
   and find the work for which they are best prepared.
2. Lack of intensified concentration and the disposition not to put more into their work than they
   expect to get out of it.
3. Lack of moral self-control.

Dr. Fitzgerald has analyzed, in person, more than
15,000 men and women. Many of the largest corpora-
tions of the middle West will not employ a man for any
important position until he has been analyzed by Dr.
Fitzgerald. He has taken men from the bookkeeper's
desk and enabled them to become successful execu-
tives. He has converted clerks into managers in much
less time than is ordinarily required, merely by having
started them in the right direction, through accurate
personal analysis.

I mention these details concerning Dr. Fitzgerald's
work because I want you to feel that my own experience, as stated in this article, is not mere conjecture
on my part—that it is authentic and that it has the

endorsement of the world's greatest personal analyst. Bear in mind that the five chief points covered by this article have been discovered, classified, and charted from the personal analysis of 25,000 people, 10,000 of whom I have analyzed and 15,000 of whom were analyzed by Dr. Fitzgerald.

## THE FIFTH SUCCESS REQUISITE

This article ought to be of benefit to those who are about to select a vocation and those who are in the wrong vocation but wish to make a change. However, there is another class to be taken into consideration. It is represented by those who have selected the right vocation but who, nevertheless, are not succeeding. I have found the Key to Success for this class. In this Great Magic Key you will find the fifth and last of the success rules which I have discovered in my vocational work.

In presenting to you this key let me first explain that it is no invention of mine.

This Great Magic Key is a most wonderful power, yet perfectly simple of operation. So simple that most people have failed to make use of it. We human beings are too prone to look askance at so simple a formula for success—a formula which will open the door to health and wealth; yet, such a formula is the Great Magic Key.

Through the Great Magic Key we have unlocked the secret doors to all of the world's great inventions. Through its magic powers all of our great geniuses have been produced. We will suppose that you desire a better position. The Great Magic Key will help you attain it! Through its use Carnegie, Rockefeller, Hill, Harriman, Morgan, and Guggenheim have accumulated millions of dollars in material wealth.

You ask—"What is this Great Magic Key?"

And I answer with one word: CONCENTRATION!

To stop here would be insufficient. You must know how to use this Great Magic Key! First, let me tell you that AMBITION and DESIRE are the great dynamic powers which you must summon to the aid of CONCENTRATION. They form the lock which this great key fits. Without ambition and desire the Great Magic Key is useless. The reason that so few people use the key is that most people lack ambition!

Desire whatever you may, and if your desire is strong enough the Great Magic Key of CONCENTRATION will help you attain it, if the object of your desire is something which it is humanly possible for you to attain.

There are learned men of science who tell us that the wonderful powers of prayer itself operate through the principle of CONCENTRATION, plus faith and strong DESIRE!

I am making no attempt to associate the Great Magic Key with occultism or religion. I am treating it from the ordinary layman's viewpoint. I am dealing with it from actual knowledge that I have gained in carefully analyzing and charting over ten thousand people.

We will assume that you are skeptical of the powers of CONCENTRATION and DESIRE. Let's put these powers to the test, through a concrete example, for unless we do this it would be just like telling you to be honest without telling you how to be honest.

## HOW TO CONCENTRATE

First, you must do away with skepticism and doubt! No unbeliever ever enjoyed the benefits of these great powers. You must believe in the test which I am going to ask you to make. You must let no feeling of unbelief creep in.

Now we will suppose that you have thought of becoming a great writer, or a great public speaker, or a great business executive, or a great advertising manager. Suppose we take the latter as the subject of this test. But remember that if you expect results you must follow instructions to the letter.

Take a plain piece of paper, ordinary letter size, and write on it in large letters—the largest it will carry—these words: I AM GOING TO BECOME

A SUCCESSFUL ADVERTISING MANAGER BECAUSE THIS WILL ENABLE ME TO RENDER THE WORLD A USEFUL SERVICE—AND BECAUSE IT WILL PROVIDE ME WITH THE NECESSARY MATERIAL THINGS OF LIFE!

I WILL CONCENTRATE ON THIS DESIRE FOR TEN MINUTES DAILY, JUST BEFORE RETIRING AND JUST AFTER RISING.

. . . . . . . . . . . . . . . . . . . . . . . . . . . . . . . . . . . . . . . . . . . . .

*(Sign your name.)*

If you are not good at lettering just clip out the foregoing, sign it, and place where you will read it just before retiring and just after getting up each day. Do exactly as you have pledged yourself to do, for at least ten days.

Now when you come to do your "CONCENTRATING" this is the way to go about it: Look ahead three, five, ten, or even fifteen years from now and see yourself in a position as advertising manager paying a big salary. See the happy faces of your loved ones—maybe a wife and babies—maybe a mother with silvery hair. Be a dreamer if you choose to call it that, but be also a "doer"! The world needs this combination of "dreamer-doers." They are the Lincolns, Grants, Edisons, Hills, Carnegies, Vanderlips, and Schwabs.

See yourself laying aside a "nest-egg" for a rainy day. See yourself in your motor car which you will be able to afford. See yourself in your own cozy little home that you will own. See yourself a person of influence in the business world.

See yourself INCREASING IN VALUE AND EARNING STILL MORE MONEY as you grow older. See yourself engaged in a line of work where you will not fear the loss of a job when the gray hairs begin to put in their appearance.

Paint this picture through the powers of your imagination, and lo! it will turn into Desire. Use this Desire as the chief object of your CONCENTRATION, and see what happens!

It may take longer than ten days for you to master this lesson in CONCENTRATION. Again it may take only one day. That will depend upon how well you perform the task.

You now have the secret of the Great Magic Key!

It will unlock the door to whatever position in life you want, if that position is one that you are prepared by nature and education to fill. It will make of you a better citizen and show you the road to true happiness if the object of your CONCENTRATION is a worthy one.

Use this Great Key with intelligence! Use it only for the attainment of worthy purposes, and it will give you the things of life for which your heart may crave. So simple, so easy of application, yet so MARVELOUS IN RESULTS! Try it! Begin right now. Forget the mistakes you have made in the past. Start all over again, and make the next five or ten years tell a story of human accomplishment in whatever line of work your calling may have placed you, that you will not be ashamed of—that the future generations of your family will be PROUD OF!

MAKE A NAME FOR YOURSELF THROUGH AMBITION, DESIRE, AND CONCENTRATION!

Vocational guidance has not yet become a universally accepted science. It may never be accepted as a science by everyone, but this does not preclude a person from using common sense in selecting a vocation. The trouble is, too many people act on a "hunch." If you are engaged in work in which you are not succeeding, take inventory of yourself and see if you cannot locate the trouble. The chances are that you can. Just apply common sense in selecting a life work. You may not be able to analyze yourself as well as a man who has many years of experience could do, therefore, if you have any doubts place yourself in the hands of a man who is experienced in analyzing men. He will undoubtedly see your weak spots more quickly than you could. Few of us can be our own best critics because we are inclined to overlook our weaknesses or place too little importance on them.

There are but few, if any, ironclad rules to follow in the selection of a vocation that would apply in every case. Probably these come as near being applicable in all cases as is possible: **Be sure you love the vocation you adopt.** Be sure you are enthusiastic over it and that you intend to stick to it. Be sure you are prepared, educationally, for the work you select. Be sure the vocation is one in which you can render a service that is beneficial to humanity. Be sure the work is permanent. Be sure that it is work that will not impair your health.

Let me summarize the five chief requisites for success, so you will not forget them. They are—first, Self-confidence; second, Enthusiasm; third, Working with a "chief aim"; fourth, Performing more work than you are paid for; fifth, Concentration, backed by desire and unwavering faith. By a reasonably intelligent application of these qualities you can become master of your own career.

Finally, I wish to leave this thought with you. It has been my constant companion through life. It has supported my tired legs when they would otherwise have allowed me to fall by the wayside. It is this:

"EVERY ADVERSITY IS, IN REALITY, A BLESSING IN DISGUISE. THE UNIVERSITY OF HARD KNOCKS SENDS FORTH ITS

GRADUATES TO FIGHT LIFE'S BATTLES, WITH PLENTY OF STRENGTH TO OVERCOME EVERY OBSTACLE THAT MAY CONFRONT THEM. FROM EVERY FAILURE WE MAY LEARN A GREAT LESSON IF WE WILL. SOMEWHERE IN THE WORLD **YOUR** PLACE IS WAITING FOR YOU. THROUGH PERSISTENCE AND INTELLIGENT EFFORT YOU WILL EVENTUALLY FIND IT. YOU WILL NEVER BE DEFEATED IN YOUR LIFE'S PURPOSE IF YOU KEEP FAITH IN THE ONLY PERSON IN THE WORLD WHO CONTROLS YOUR DESTINY—**YOURSELF!**"

# HOW TO OUTWIT THE SIX GHOSTS OF FEAR

Excerpted from *Think and Grow Rich*

Before you can put any portion of this philosophy into successful use, your mind must be prepared to receive it. The preparation is not difficult. It begins with study, analysis, and understanding of three enemies which you shall have to clear out. These are **indecision, doubt, and fear!** The members of this unholy trio are closely related; where one is found, the other two are close at hand.

**Indecision** is the seedling of fear! Remember this, as you read. Indecision crystallizes into **doubt**; the two blend and become **fear!** The "blending" process often is slow. This is one reason why these three enemies are so dangerous. They germinate and grow *without their presence being observed.*

The purpose of this chapter is to turn the spotlight

of attention upon the cause and the cure of the six basic fears. Before we can master an enemy, we must know its name, its habits, and its place of abode. As you read, analyze yourself carefully, and determine which, if any, of the six common fears have attached themselves to you.

Do not be deceived by the habits of these subtle enemies. Sometimes they remain hidden in the subconscious mind, where they are difficult to locate, and still more difficult to eliminate.

## THE SIX BASIC FEARS

There are six basic fears, with some combination of which every human suffers at one time or another. Most people are fortunate if they do not suffer from the entire six. Named in the order of their most common appearance, they are:—

The fear of **POVERTY**
The fear of **CRITICISM**
The fear of **ILL HEALTH**
(*the above three are at the bottom of most of one's worries*)
The fear of **LOSS OF LOVE OF SOMEONE**
The fear of **OLD AGE**
The fear of **DEATH**

All other fears are of minor importance; they can be grouped under these six headings.

The prevalence of these fears, as a curse to the world, runs in cycles. For almost six years, while the depression was on, we floundered in the cycle of fear of poverty. During the world war, we were in the cycle of fear of death. Just following the war, we were in the cycle of fear of ill health, as evidenced by the epidemic of disease which spread itself all over the world.

*Fears are nothing more than states of mind.* One's state of mind is subject to control and direction. Physicians, as everyone knows, are less subject to attack by disease than ordinary laymen, for the reason that physicians do not fear disease. Physicians, without fear or hesitation, have been known to physically contact hundreds of people, daily, who were suffering from such contagious diseases as small-pox, without becoming infected. Their immunity against the disease consisted, largely, if not solely, in their absolute lack of fear.

Man can create nothing which he does not first conceive in the form of an impulse of thought. Following this statement, comes another of still greater importance, namely man's thought impulses begin immediately to translate themselves into their physical equivalent, whether those thoughts are voluntary or involuntary. Thought impulses which are picked up through the ether, by mere chance (thoughts which have been released by other minds) may determine one's financial, business, professional, or social destiny just as surely as do the thought impulses which one creates by intent and design.

We are here laying the foundation for the presentation of a fact of great importance to the person who does not understand why some people appear to be "lucky" while others of equal or greater ability, training, experience, and brain capacity, seem destined to ride with misfortune. This fact may be explained by the statement that *every human being has the ability to completely control his own mind*, and with this control, obviously, every person may open his mind to the tramp thought impulses which are being released by other brains, or close the doors tightly and admit only thought impulses of his own choice.

Nature has endowed man with absolute control over but one thing, and that is thought. This fact, coupled with the additional fact that everything which man creates begins in the form of a thought, leads one very near to the principle by which fear may be mastered.

If it is true that all thought has a tendency to clothe itself in its physical equivalent (and this is true, beyond any reasonable room for doubt), it is equally true that thought impulses of fear and poverty cannot be translated into terms of courage and financial gain.

The people of America began to think of poverty, following the Wall Street crash of 1929. Slowly, but surely that mass thought was crystallized into its physical equivalent, which was known as a "depression." This had to happen; it is in conformity with the laws of Nature.

## THE FEAR OF POVERTY

There can be no compromise between poverty and riches! The two roads that lead to poverty and riches travel in opposite directions. If you want riches, you must refuse to accept any circumstance that leads toward poverty. (The word "riches" is here used in its broadest sense, meaning financial, spiritual, mental and material estates.) The starting point of the path that leads to riches is desire. In chapter two, you received full instructions for the proper use of desire. In this chapter, on fear, you have complete instructions for preparing your mind to make practical use of desire.

Here, then, is the place to give yourself a challenge which will definitely determine how much of this philosophy you have absorbed. Here is the point at which you can turn prophet and foretell, accurately, what the future holds in store for you. If, after reading this chapter, you are willing to accept poverty, you may as well make up your mind to receive poverty. This is one decision you cannot avoid.

If you demand riches, determine what form, and

how much will be required to satisfy you. You know the road that leads to riches. You have been given a road map which, if followed, will keep you on that road. If you neglect to make the start, or stop before you arrive, no one will be to blame but you. This responsibility is yours. No alibi will save you from accepting the responsibility if you now fail or refuse to demand riches of Life, because the acceptance calls for but one thing— incidentally, the only thing you can control—and that is a state of mind. A state of mind is something that one assumes. It cannot be purchased; it must be created.

Fear of poverty is a state of mind, nothing else! But it is sufficient to destroy one's chances of achievement in any undertaking, a truth which became painfully evident during the depression.

This fear paralyzes the faculty of reason, destroys the faculty of imagination, kills off self-reliance, undermines enthusiasm, discourages initiative, leads to uncertainty of purpose, encourages procrastination, wipes out enthusiasm and makes self-control an impossibility. It takes the charm from one's personality, destroys the possibility of accurate thinking, diverts concentration of effort; it masters persistence, turns the will-power into nothingness, destroys ambition, beclouds the memory and invites failure in every conceivable form; it kills love and assassinates the finer emotions of the heart, discourages friendship and invites disaster in a hundred forms, leads to sleeplessness, misery and unhappiness—and all this despite the obvious truth that we live in a world of over-abundance of everything the heart could desire, with nothing standing between us and our desires, excepting lack of a definite purpose.

The Fear of Poverty is, without doubt, the most destructive of the six basic fears. It has been placed at the head of the list, because it is the most difficult to master. Considerable courage is required to state the truth about the origin of this fear, and still greater courage to accept the truth after it has been stated. The fear of poverty grew out of man's inherited tendency to prey upon his fellow man economically. Nearly all animals lower than man are motivated by instinct, but their capacity to "think" is limited, therefore, they prey upon one another physically. Man, with his superior sense of intuition, with the capacity to think and to reason, does not eat his fellow man bodily, he gets more satisfaction out of "eating" him financially. Man is so avaricious that every conceivable law has been passed to safeguard him from his fellow man.

Of all the ages of the world, of which we know anything, the age in which we live seems to be one that is outstanding because of man's money-madness. A man is considered less than the dust of the earth, unless he can display a fat bank account; but if he has money—never mind how he acquired it—he is a "king" or a "big shot"; he is above the law, he rules in politics, he dominates in business, and the whole world about him bows in respect when he passes.

Nothing brings man so much suffering and humility as poverty! Only those who have experienced poverty understand the full meaning of this.

It is no wonder that man *fears* poverty. Through a long line of inherited experiences man has learned, for sure, that some men cannot be trusted, where matters of money and earthly possessions are concerned. This is a rather stinging indictment, the worst part of it being that it is true.

The majority of people, if asked what they fear most, would reply, "I fear nothing." The reply would be inaccurate, because few people realize that they are bound, handicapped, whipped spiritually and physically through some form of fear. So subtle and deeply seated is the emotion of fear that one may go through life burdened with it, never recognizing its presence. Only a courageous analysis will disclose the presence of this universal enemy. When you begin such an analysis, search deeply into your character. Here is a list of the symptoms for which you should look:

## Symptoms of the Fear of Poverty

INDIFFERENCE: Commonly expressed through lack of ambition; willingness to tolerate poverty;

acceptance of whatever compensation life may offer without protest; mental and physical laziness; lack of initiative, imagination, enthusiasm and self-control.

**INDECISION:** The habit of permitting others to do one's thinking. Staying "on the fence."

**DOUBT:** Generally expressed through alibis and excuses designed to cover up, explain away, or apologize for one's failures, sometimes expressed in the form of envy of those who are successful, or by criticising them.

**WORRY:** Usually expressed by finding fault with others, a tendency to spend beyond one's income, neglect of personal appearance, scowling and frowning; intemperance in the use of alcoholic drink, sometimes through the use of narcotics; nervousness, lack of poise, self-consciousness and lack of self-reliance.

**OVER-CAUTION:** The habit of looking for the negative side of every circumstance, thinking and talking of possible failure instead of concentrating upon the means of succeeding. Knowing all the roads to disaster, but never searching for the plans to avoid failure. Waiting for "the right time" to begin putting ideas and plans into action, until the waiting becomes a permanent habit. Remembering those who have failed, and forgetting those who have succeeded. Seeing the hole in the doughnut, but overlooking the doughnut. Pessimism, leading to indigestion, poor elimination, auto-intoxication, bad breath and bad disposition.

PROCRASTINATION: The habit of putting off until tomorrow that which should have been done last year. Spending enough time in creating alibis and excuses to have done the job. This symptom is closely related to over-caution, doubt and worry. Refusal to accept responsibility when it can be avoided. Willingness to compromise rather than put up a stiff fight. Compromising with difficulties instead of harnessing and using them as stepping stones to advancement. Bargaining with Life for a penny, instead of demanding prosperity, opulence, riches, contentment and happiness. Planning what to do if and when overtaken by failure, instead of burning all bridges and making retreat impossible. Weakness of, and often total lack of self-confidence, definiteness of purpose, self-control, initiative, enthusiasm, ambition, thrift and sound reasoning ability. Expecting poverty instead of demanding riches. Association with those who accept poverty instead of seeking the company of those who demand and receive riches.

## MONEY TALKS!

Some will ask, "Why did you write a book about money? Why measure riches in dollars, alone?" Some will believe, and rightly so, that there are other forms of riches more desirable than money. Yes, there are riches which cannot be measured in terms of dollars, but there are millions of people who will say, "Give me all the money I need, and I will find everything else I want."

The major reason why I wrote on how to get money is the fact that the world has but lately passed through an experience that left millions of men and women paralyzed with the fear of poverty.

## THE FEAR OF CRITICISM

Just how man originally came by this fear, no one can state definitely, but one thing is certain—he has it in a highly developed form. Some believe that this fear made its appearance about the time that politics became a "profession." Others believe it can be traced to the age when women first began to concern themselves with "styles" in wearing apparel.

This author, being neither a humorist nor a prophet, is inclined to attribute the basic fear of criticism to that part of man's inherited nature which prompts him not only to take away his fellow man's goods and wares, but to justify his action by criticism of his fellow man's character. It is a well-known fact that a thief will criticise the man from whom he steals—that politicians seek office, not by displaying their own virtues and qualifications, but by attempting to besmirch their opponents.

The astute manufacturers of clothing have not been slow to capitalize on this basic fear of criticism, with which all mankind has been cursed. Every season the styles in many articles of wearing apparel change. Who establishes the styles? Certainly not the purchaser of clothing, but the manufacturer. Why does he change the styles so often? The answer is obvious. He changes the styles so he can sell more clothes.

For the same reason the manufacturers of automobiles (with a few rare and very sensible exceptions) change styles of models every season. No man wants to drive an automobile which is not of the latest style, although the older model may actually be the better car.

We have been describing the manner in which people behave under the influence of fear of criticism as applied to the small and petty things of life. Let us now examine human behavior when this fear affects people in connection with the more important events of human relationship. Take for example practically any person who has reached the age of "mental maturity" (from thirty-five to forty years of age, as a general average), and if you could read the secret thoughts of his mind, you would find a very decided disbelief in most of the fables taught by the majority of the dogmatists and theologians a few decades back.

Not often, however, will you find a person who has the courage to openly state his belief on this subject. Most people will, if pressed far enough, tell a lie rather than admit that they do not believe the stories associated with that form of religion which held people in bondage prior to the age of scientific discovery and education.

Why does the average person, even in this day of enlightenment, shy away from denying his belief in the fables which were the basis of most of the religions a few decades ago? The answer is, "because of the fear of criticism." Men and women have been burned at the stake for daring to express disbelief in ghosts. It is no wonder we have inherited a consciousness which makes us fear criticism. The time was, and not so far in the past, when criticism carried severe punishments—it still does in some countries.

The fear of criticism robs man of his initiative, destroys his power of imagination, limits his individuality, takes away his self-reliance, and does him damage in a hundred other ways.

Criticism is the one form of service, of which everyone has too much. Everyone has a stock of it which is handed out, gratis, whether called for or not. One's nearest relatives often are the worst offenders. It should be recognized as a crime (in reality it is a crime of the worst nature) for any parent to build inferiority complexes in the mind of a child, through unnecessary criticism. Employers who understand human nature get the best there is not by criticism, but by constructive suggestion. Parents may accomplish the same results with their children. Criticism will plant fear in the human heart, or resentment, but it will not build love or affection.

## Symptoms of the Fear of Criticism

This fear is almost as universal as the fear of poverty, and its effects are just as fatal to personal achievement, mainly because this fear destroys initiative, and discourages the use of imagination.

The major symptoms of the fear are:

**SELF-CONSCIOUSNESS:** Generally expressed through nervousness, timidity in conversation and in meeting strangers, awkward movement of the hands and limbs, shifting of the eyes.

**LACK OF POISE:** Expressed through lack of voice control, nervousness in the presence of others, poor posture of body, poor memory.

**PERSONALITY:** Lacking in firmness of decision, personal charm, and ability to express opinions definitely. The habit of sidestepping issues instead of meeting them squarely. Agreeing with others without careful examination of their opinions.

**INFERIORITY COMPLEX:** The habit of expressing self-approval by word of mouth and by actions, as a means of covering up a feeling of inferiority. Using "big words" to impress others (often without knowing the real meaning of the words). Imitating others in dress, speech and manners. Boasting of imaginary achievements. This sometimes gives a surface appearance of a feeling of superiority.

**EXTRAVAGANCE:** The habit of trying to "keep up with the Joneses," spending beyond one's income.

**LACK OF INITIATIVE:** Failure to embrace opportunities for self-advancement, fear to express opinions, lack of confidence in one's own ideas, giving evasive answers to questions asked by superiors, hesitancy of manner and speech, deceit in both words and deeds.

**LACK OF AMBITION:** Mental and physical laziness, lack of self-assertion, slowness in reaching decisions, easily influenced by others, the habit of criticising others behind their backs and flattering them to their faces, the habit of accepting defeat without protest, quitting an undertaking when opposed by others, suspicious of other people without cause, lacking in tactfulness of manner and speech, unwillingness to accept the blame for mistakes.

## THE FEAR OF ILL HEALTH

This fear may be traced to both physical and social heredity. It is closely associated, as to its origin, with the causes of fear of Old Age and the fear of Death, because it leads one closely to the border of "terrible worlds" of which man knows not, but concerning which he has been taught some discomforting stories. The opinion is somewhat general, also, that certain unethical people engaged in the business of "selling health" have had not a little to do with keeping alive the fear of ill health.

In the main, man fears ill health because of the terrible pictures which have been planted in his mind of what may happen if death should overtake him. He also fears it because of the economic toll which it may claim.

A reputable physician estimated that 75% of all people who visit physicians for professional service are suffering with hypochondria (imaginary illness). It has been shown most convincingly that the fear of disease, even where there is not the slightest cause for fear, often produces the physical symptoms of the disease feared.

Powerful and mighty is the human mind! It builds or it destroys.

Playing upon this common weakness of fear of ill health, dispensers of patent medicines have reaped fortunes. This form of imposition upon credulous humanity became so prevalent some twenty years ago that

*Colliers' Weekly Magazine* conducted a bitter campaign against some of the worst offenders in the patent medicine business.

During the "flu" epidemic which broke out during the world war, the mayor of New York City took drastic steps to check the damage which people were doing themselves through their inherent fear of ill health. He called in the newspaper men and said to them, "Gentlemen, I feel it necessary to ask you not to publish any *scare headlines* concerning the 'flu' epidemic. Unless you cooperate with me, we will have a situation which we cannot control." The newspapers quit publishing stories about the "flu," and within one month the epidemic had been successfully checked.

Through a series of experiments conducted some years ago, it was proved that people may be made ill by suggestion. We conducted this experiment by causing three acquaintances to visit the "victims," each of whom asked the question, "What ails you? You look terribly ill." The first questioner usually provoked a grin, and a nonchalant "Oh, nothing, I'm all right," from the victim. The second questioner usually was answered with the statement, "I don't know exactly, but I do feel badly." The third questioner was usually met with the frank admission that the victim was actually feeling ill.

There is overwhelming evidence that disease sometimes begins in the form of negative thought impulse.

Such an impulse may be passed from one mind to another, by suggestion, or created by an individual in his own mind.

Doctors send patients into new climates for their health, because a change of "mental attitude" is necessary. The seed of fear of ill health lives in every human mind. Worry, fear, discouragement, disappointment in love and business affairs, cause this seed to germinate and grow. The recent business depression kept the doctors on the run, because every form of negative thinking may cause ill health.

## Symptoms of the Fear of Ill Health

The symptoms of this almost universal fear are:

AUTO-SUGGESTION: The habit of negative use of self-suggestion by looking for, and expecting to find the symptoms of all kinds of disease. "Enjoying" imaginary illness and speaking of it as being real. The habit of trying all "fads" and "isms" recommended by others as having therapeutic value. Talking to others of operations, accidents and other forms of illness. Experimenting with diets, physical exercises, reducing systems, without professional guidance. Trying home remedies, patent medicines and "quack" remedies.

HYPOCHONDRIA: The habit of talking of

illness, concentrating the mind upon disease, and expecting its appearance until a nervous break occurs. Nothing that comes in bottles can cure this condition. It is brought on by negative thinking and nothing but positive thought can effect a cure. Hypochondria (a medical term for imaginary disease) is said to do as much damage on occasion, as the disease one fears might do. Most so-called cases of "nerves" come from imaginary illness.

**EXERCISE:** Fear of ill health often interferes with proper physical exercise, and results in overweight, by causing one to avoid outdoor life.

**SUSCEPTIBILITY:** Fear of ill health breaks down Nature's body resistance, and creates a favorable condition for any form of disease one may contact. The fear of ill health often is related to the fear of Poverty, especially in the case of the hypochondriac, who constantly worries about the possibility of having to pay doctor's bills, hospital bills, etc. This type of person spends much time preparing for sickness, talking about death, saving money for cemetery lots, and burial expenses, etc.

**SELF-CODDLING:** The habit of making a bid for sympathy, using imaginary illness as the lure. (People often resort to this trick to avoid work.) The habit of feigning illness to cover plain laziness, or to serve as an alibi for lack of ambition.

INTEMPERANCE: The habit of using alcohol or narcotics to destroy pains such as headaches, neuralgia, etc., instead of eliminating the cause.

## THE FEAR OF LOSS OF LOVE

The original source of this inherent fear needs but little description, because it obviously grew out of man's polygamous habit of stealing his fellow man's mate, and his habit of taking liberties with her whenever he could.

Jealousy, and other similar forms of dementia praecox grow out of man's inherited fear of the loss of love of someone. This fear is the most painful of all the six basic fears. It probably plays more havoc with the body and mind than any of the other basic fears, as it often leads to permanent insanity.

### Symptoms of the Fear of Loss of Love

The distinguishing symptoms of this fear are:

JEALOUSY: The habit of being suspicious of friends and loved ones without any reasonable evidence of sufficient grounds. (Jealousy is a form of dementia praecox which sometimes becomes violent without the slightest cause.) The habit of accusing wife or husband of infidelity without grounds. General suspicion of everyone, absolute faith in no one.

**FAULT FINDING:** The habit of finding fault with friends, relatives, business associates and loved ones upon the slightest provocation, or without any cause whatsoever.

**GAMBLING:** The habit of gambling, stealing, cheating, and otherwise taking hazardous chances to provide money for loved ones, with the belief that love can be bought. The habit of spending beyond one's means, or incurring debts, to provide gifts for loved ones, with the object of making a favorable showing. Insomnia, nervousness, lack of persistence, weakness of will, lack of self-control, lack of self-reliance, bad temper.

## THE FEAR OF OLD AGE

In the main, this fear grows out of two sources. First, the thought that old age may bring with it poverty. Secondly, and by far the most common source of origin, from false and cruel teachings of the past which have been too well mixed with "fire and brimstone," and other bogies cunningly designed to enslave man through fear.

In the basic fear of old age, man has two very sound reasons for his apprehension—one growing out of his distrust of his fellow man, who may seize whatever worldly goods he may possess, and the other arising from the terrible pictures of the world beyond, which were planted in his mind, through social heredity before he came into full possession of his mind.

The possibility of ill health, which is more common as people grow older, is also a contributing cause of this common fear of old age. Eroticism also enters into the cause of the fear of old age, as no man cherishes the thought of diminishing sex attraction.

The most common cause of fear of old age is associated with the possibility of poverty. "Poorhouse" is not a pretty word. It throws a chill into the mind of every person who faces the possibility of having to spend his declining years on a poor farm.

Another contributing cause of the fear of old age is the possibility of loss of freedom and independence, as old age may bring with it the loss of both physical and economic freedom.

## Symptoms of the Fear of Old Age

The commonest symptoms of this fear are:

The tendency to slow down and develop an inferiority complex at the age of mental maturity, around the age of forty, falsely believing oneself to be "slipping" because of age. (The truth is that man's most useful years, mentally and spiritually, are those between forty and sixty.)

The habit of speaking apologetically of one's self as "being old" merely because one has reached the age of forty, or fifty, instead of reversing the rule and expressing gratitude for having reached the age of wisdom and understanding.

The habit of killing off initiative, imagination, and self-reliance by falsely believing one's self too old to exercise these qualities. The habit of the man or woman of forty dressing with the aim of trying to appear much younger, and affecting mannerisms of youth; thereby inspiring ridicule by both friends and strangers.

## THE FEAR OF DEATH

To some this is the cruelest of all the basic fears. The reason is obvious. The terrible pangs of fear associated with the thought of death, in the majority of cases, may be charged directly to religious fanaticism. So-called "heathen" are less afraid of death than the more "civilized." For hundreds of millions of years man has been asking the still-unanswered questions, "whence" and "whither." Where did I come from, and where am I going?

During the darker ages of the past, the more cunning and crafty were not slow to offer the answer to these questions, for a price. Witness, now, the major source of origin of the fear of death.

"Come into my tent, embrace my faith, accept my dogmas, and I will give you a ticket that will admit you straightaway into heaven when you die," cries a leader of sectarianism. "Remain out of my tent," says the same leader, "and may the devil take you and burn you throughout eternity."

Eternity is a long time. Fire is a terrible thing. The thought of eternal punishment, with fire, not only causes man to fear death, it often causes him to lose his reason. It destroys interest in life and makes happiness impossible.

During my research, I reviewed a book entitled *A Catalogue of the Gods*, in which were listed the 30,000 gods which man has worshiped. Think of it! Thirty thousand of them, represented by everything from a crawfish to a man. It is little wonder that men have become frightened at the approach of death.

While the religious leader may not be able to provide safe conduct into heaven, nor, by lack of such provision, allow the unfortunate to descend into hell, the possibility of the latter seems so terrible that the very thought of it lays hold of the imagination in such a realistic way that it paralyzes reason, and sets up the fear of death.

In truth, no man knows, and no man has ever known,

what heaven or hell is like, nor does any man know if either place actually exists. This very lack of positive knowledge opens the door of the human mind to the charlatan so he may enter and control that mind with his stock of legerdemain and various brands of pious fraud and trickery.

The fear of death is not as common now as it was during the age when there were no great colleges and universities. Men of science have turned the spotlight of truth upon the world, and this truth is rapidly freeing men and women from this terrible fear of death. The young men and young women who attend the colleges and universities are not easily impressed by "fire" and "brimstone." Through the aid of biology, astronomy, geology, and other related sciences, the fears of the dark ages which gripped the minds of men and destroyed their reason have been dispelled.

Insane asylums are filled with men and women who have gone mad, because of the fear of death.

This fear is useless. Death will come, no matter what anyone may think about it. Accept it as a necessity, and pass the thought out of your mind. It must be a necessity, or it would not come to all. Perhaps it is not as bad as it has been pictured.

The entire world is made up of only two things, energy and matter. In elementary physics we learn that neither matter nor energy (the only two realities known to man) can be created or destroyed. Both matter and energy can be transformed, but neither can be destroyed.

Life is energy, if it is anything. If neither energy nor matter can be destroyed, of course life cannot be destroyed. Life, like other forms of energy, may be passed through various processes of transition, or change, but it cannot be destroyed. Death is mere transition.

If death is not mere change, or transition, then nothing comes after death except a long, eternal, peaceful sleep, and sleep is nothing to be feared. Thus you may wipe out, forever, the fear of Death.

## Symptoms of the Fear of Death

The general symptoms of this fear are:

The habit of thinking about dying instead of making the most of life, due, generally, to lack of purpose, or lack of a suitable occupation. This fear is more prevalent among the aged, but sometimes the more youthful are victims of it. The greatest of all remedies for the fear of death is a burning desire for achievement, backed by useful service to others. A busy person seldom has time to think about dying. He finds life too thrilling to worry about death. Sometimes the fear of death is closely associated with the Fear of Poverty, where one's death would leave loved ones poverty-stricken. In other cases, the fear of death is caused by illness and the consequent breaking down of physical body resistance. The commonest causes of the fear of death are: ill health, poverty, lack of appropriate occupation, disappointment over love, insanity, religious fanaticism.

## OLD MAN WORRY

Worry is a state of mind based upon fear. It works slowly, but persistently. It is insidious and subtle. Step by step it "digs itself in" until it paralyzes one's reasoning faculty, destroys self-confidence and initiative. Worry is a form of sustained fear caused by indecision, therefore it is a state of mind which can be controlled.

An unsettled mind is helpless. Indecision makes an unsettled mind. Most individuals lack the will-power to reach decisions promptly, and to stand by them after they have been made, even during normal business conditions. During periods of economic unrest (such as the world recently experienced), the individual is handicapped, not alone by his inherent nature to be slow at reaching decisions, but he is influenced by the indecision of others around him who have created a state of "mass indecision."

During the depression the whole atmosphere, all over the world, was filled with "Fearenza" and "Worryitis," the two mental disease germs which began to spread themselves after the Wall Street frenzy in 1929. There is only one known antidote for these germs; it is the habit of prompt and firm decision. Moreover, it is an antidote which every individual must apply for himself.

The six basic fears become translated into a state of worry, through indecision. Relieve yourself, forever of the fear of death, by reaching a decision to accept death as an inescapable event. Whip the fear of poverty by reaching a decision to get along with whatever wealth you can accumulate without worry. Put your foot upon the neck of the fear of criticism by reaching a decision not to worry about what other people think, do, or say. Eliminate the fear of old age by reaching a decision to accept it, not as a handicap, but as a great blessing which carries with it wisdom, self-control, and understanding not known to youth. Acquit yourself of the fear of ill health by the decision to forget symptoms. Master the fear of loss of love by reaching a decision to get along without love, if that is necessary.

Kill the habit of worry, in all its forms, by reaching a general, blanket decision that nothing which life has to offer is worth the price of worry. With this decision will come poise, peace of mind, and calmness of thought which will bring happiness.

A man whose mind is filled with fear not only destroys his own chances of intelligent action, but, he transmits these destructive vibrations to the minds of all who come into contact with him, and destroys, also, their chances.

Even a dog or a horse knows when its master lacks courage; moreover, a dog or a horse will pick up the vibrations of fear thrown off by its master, and behave accordingly. Lower down the line of intelligence in the animal kingdom, one finds this same capacity to pick up the vibrations of fear. A honey-bee immediately senses fear in the mind of a person—for reasons unknown, a bee will sting the person whose mind is releasing vibrations of fear, much more readily than it will molest the person whose mind registers no fear.

The vibrations of fear pass from one mind to another just as quickly and as surely as the sound of the human voice passes from the broadcasting station to the receiving set of a radio—and by the self-same medium.

*Mental telepathy is a reality.* Thoughts pass from one mind to another, voluntarily, whether or not this fact is recognized by either the person releasing the thoughts, or the persons who pick up those thoughts.

The person who gives expression, by word of mouth, to negative or destructive thoughts is practically certain to experience the results of those words in the form of a destructive "kick-back." The release of destructive thought impulses, alone, without the aid of words, produces also a "kick-back" in more ways than one. First of all, and perhaps most important to be remembered, the person who releases thoughts of a destructive nature must suffer damage through the breaking down of the faculty of creative imagination. Secondly, the presence in the mind of any destructive emotion develops a negative personality which repels people, and often converts them into antagonists. The third source of damage to the person who entertains or releases negative thoughts, lies in this significant fact—these thought-impulses are not only damaging to others, but they imbed themselves in the subconscious mind of the person releasing them, and there become a part of his character.

One is never through with a thought, merely by releasing it. When a thought is released, it spreads in every direction, through the medium of the ether, but it also plants itself *permanently* in the subconscious mind of *the person releasing it.*

Your business in life is presumably to achieve success. To be successful, you must find peace of mind, acquire the material needs of life, and above all, attain happiness. All of these evidences of success begin in the form of thought impulses.

You may control your own mind; you have the power to feed it whatever thought impulses you choose. With this privilege goes also the responsibility of using it constructively. You are the master of your own earthly destiny just as surely as you have the power to control your own thoughts. You may influence, direct, and eventually control your own environment, making your life what you want it to be—or, you may neglect to exercise the privilege which is yours, to make your life to order, thus casting yourself upon the broad sea of "Circumstance" where you will be tossed hither and yon, like a chip on the waves of the ocean.

# HOW TO PROTECT YOURSELF AGAINST NEGATIVE INFLUENCES

Excerpted from *Think and Grow Rich*

To protect yourself against negative influences, whether of your own making, or the result of the activities of negative people around you, recognize that you have a will-power, and put it into constant use, until it builds a wall of immunity against negative influences in your own mind.

Recognize the fact that you, and every other human being, are, by nature, lazy, indifferent, and susceptible to all suggestions which harmonize with your weaknesses.

Recognize that you are, by nature, susceptible to all the six basic fears, and set up habits for the purpose of counteracting all these fears.

Recognize that negative influences often work on you through your subconscious mind, therefore they are difficult to detect, and keep your mind closed against all people who depress or discourage you in any way.

Deliberately seek the company of people who influence you to think and act for yourself.

Do not expect troubles as they have a tendency not to disappoint.

*Without doubt, the most common weakness of all human beings is the habit of leaving their minds open to the negative influence of other people.* This weakness is all the more damaging, because most people do not recognize that they are cursed by it, and many who acknowledge it, neglect or refuse to correct the evil until it becomes an uncontrollable part of their daily habits.

To aid those who wish to see themselves as they really are, the following list of questions has been prepared. Read the questions and state your answers aloud, so you can hear your own voice. This will make it easier for you to be truthful with yourself.

If you answer all these questions truthfully, you know more about yourself than the majority of people. Study the questions carefully, come back to them once each week for several months, and be astounded at the amount of additional knowledge of great value to yourself, you will have gained by the simple method of answering the questions truthfully. If you are not certain concerning the answers to some of the questions, seek the counsel of those who know you well, especially those who have no motive in flattering you, and see yourself through their eyes. The experience will be astonishing.

## Self-Analysis Test Questions

Do you complain often of "feeling bad," and if so, what is the cause?

Do you find fault with other people at the slightest provocation?

Do you frequently make mistakes in your work, and if so, why?

Are you sarcastic and offensive in your conversation?

Do you deliberately avoid the association of anyone, and if so, why?

Do you suffer frequently with indigestion? If so, what is the cause?

Does life seem futile and the future hopeless to you? If so, why?

Do you like your occupation? If not, why?

Do you often feel self-pity, and if so why?

Are you envious of those who excel you?

To which do you devote most time, thinking of success, or of failure?

Are you gaining or losing self-confidence as you grow older?

Do you learn something of value from all mistakes? Are you permitting some relative or acquaintance to worry you? If so, why?

Are you sometimes "in the clouds" and at other times in the depths of despondency?

Who has the most inspiring influence upon you? What is the cause?

Do you tolerate negative or discouraging influences which you can avoid?

Are you careless of your personal appearance? If so, when and why?

Have you learned how to "drown your troubles" by being too busy to be annoyed by them?

Would you call yourself a "spineless weakling" if you permitted others to do your thinking for you?

Do you neglect internal bathing until auto-intoxication makes you ill-tempered and irritable?

How many preventable disturbances annoy you, and why do you tolerate them?

Do you resort to liquor, narcotics, or cigarettes to "quiet your nerves"? If so, why do you not try will-power instead?

Does anyone "nag" you, and if so, for what reason?

Do you have a definite major purpose, and if so, what is it, and what plan have you for achieving it?

Do you suffer from any of the Six Basic Fears? If so, which ones?

Have you a method by which you can shield yourself against the negative influence of others?

Do you make deliberate use of auto-suggestion to make your mind positive?

Which do you value most, your material possessions, or your privilege of controlling your own thoughts?

Are you easily influenced by others, against your own judgment?

Has today added anything of value to your stock of knowledge or state of mind?

Do you face squarely the circumstances which make you unhappy, or sidestep the responsibility?

Do you analyze all mistakes and failures and try to profit by them or, do you take the attitude that this is not your duty?

Can you name three of your most damaging weaknesses? What are you doing to correct them?

Do you encourage other people to bring their worries to you for sympathy?

Do you choose, from your daily experiences, lessons or influences which aid in your personal advancement?

Does your presence have a negative influence on other people as a rule?

What habits of other people annoy you most?

Do you form your own opinions or permit yourself to be influenced by other people?

Have you learned how to create a mental state of mind with which you can shield yourself against all discouraging influences?

Does your occupation inspire you with faith and hope?

Are you conscious of possessing spiritual forces of sufficient power to enable you to keep your mind free from all forms of fear?

Does your religion help you to keep your own mind positive?

Do you feel it your duty to share other people's worries? If so, why?

If you believe that "birds of a feather flock together" what have you learned about yourself by studying the friends whom you attract?

What connection, if any, do you see between the people with whom you associate most closely, and any unhappiness you may experience?

Could it be possible that some person whom you consider to be a friend is, in reality, your worst enemy, because of his negative influence on your mind?

By what rules do you judge who is helpful and who is damaging to you?

Are your intimate associates mentally superior or inferior to you?

How much time out of every twenty-four hours do you devote to:

- **a.** your occupation
- **b.** sleep
- **c.** play and relaxation
- **d.** acquiring useful knowledge
- **e.** plain waste

Who among your acquaintances,

- **a.** encourages you most
- **b.** cautions you most
- **c.** discourages you most
- **d.** helps you most in other ways

What is your greatest worry? Why do you tolerate it?

When others offer you free, unsolicited advice, do you accept it without question, or analyze their motive?

What, above all else, do you most desire? Do you intend to acquire it? Are you willing to subordinate all other desires for this one? How much time daily do you devote to acquiring it?

Do you change your mind often? If so, why?

Do you usually finish everything you begin?

Are you easily impressed by other people's business or professional titles, college degrees, or wealth? Are you easily influenced by what other people think or say of you?

Do you cater to people because of their social or financial status?

Whom do you believe to be the greatest person living? In what respect is this person superior to yourself?

How much time have you devoted to studying and answering these questions? (At least one day is necessary for the analysis and the answering of the entire list.)

**You have absolute control over but one thing, and that is your thoughts.** This is the most significant and inspiring of all facts known to man! It reflects man's Divine nature. This Divine prerogative is the sole means by which you may control your own destiny. If you fail to control your own mind, you may be sure you will control nothing else.

If you must be careless with your possessions, let it be in connection with material things. *Your mind is your spiritual estate!* Protect and use it with the care to which Divine Royalty is entitled. You were given a will-power for this purpose.

Unfortunately, there is no legal protection against those who, either by design or ignorance, poison the minds of others by negative suggestion. This form of destruction should be punishable by heavy legal penalties, because it may and often does destroy one's chances of acquiring material things which are protected by law.

Men with negative minds tried to convince Thomas A. Edison that he could not build a machine that would record and reproduce the human voice, "because" they said, "no one else had ever produced such a machine." Edison did not believe them. He knew that the mind could produce anything the mind could conceive and believe, and that knowledge was the thing that lifted the great Edison above the common herd.

Men with negative minds told F. W. Woolworth he would go "broke" trying to run a store on five and ten cent sales. He did not believe them. He knew that he could do anything, within reason, if he backed his plans with faith. Exercising his right to keep other men's negative suggestions out of his mind, he piled up a fortune of more than a hundred million dollars.

Men with negative minds told George Washington he could not hope to win against the vastly superior forces of the British, but he exercised his Divine right to believe, therefore this book was published under the protection of the Stars and Stripes, while the name of Lord Cornwallis has been all but forgotten.

Doubting Thomases scoffed scornfully when Henry Ford tried out his first crudely built automobile on the streets of Detroit. Some said the thing never would become practical. Others said no one would pay money for such a contraption. Ford said, "I'll belt the earth with dependable motor cars," and he did! His decision to trust his own judgment has already piled up a fortune far greater than the next five generations of his descendants can squander.

Mind control is the result of self-discipline and habit. You either control your mind or it controls you. There is no half-way compromise. The most practical of all methods for controlling the mind is the habit of keeping it busy with a definite purpose, backed by a definite plan. Study the record of any man who achieves noteworthy success, and you will observe that he has control over his own mind, moreover, that he exercises that control and directs it toward the attainment of definite objectives. Without this control, success is not possible.

# FIFTY-SEVEN

# FAMOUS ALIBIS

Excerpted from *Think and Grow Rich*

## BY OLD MAN "IF"

People who do not succeed have one distinguishing trait in common. They know *all the reasons for failure*, and have what they believe to be airtight alibis to explain away their own lack of achievement.

Some of these alibis are clever, and a few of them are justifiable by the facts. But alibis cannot be used for money. The world wants to know only one thing—have you achieved success?

A character analyst compiled a list of the most commonly used alibis. As you read the list, examine yourself carefully, and determine how many of these alibis, if any, are your own property. Remember, too, the philosophy presented in this book makes every one of these alibis obsolete.

IF I didn't have a wife and family . . .

IF I had enough "pull" . . .

IF I had money . . .

IF I had a good education . . .

IF I could get a job . . .

IF I had good health . . .

IF I only had time . . .

IF times were better . . .

IF other people understood me . . .

IF conditions around me were only different . . .

IF I could live my life over again . . .

IF I did not fear what "they" would say . . .

IF I had been given a chance . . .

IF I now had a chance . . .

IF other people didn't "have it in for me" . . .

IF nothing happens to stop me . . .

IF I were only younger . . .

IF I could only do what I want . . .

IF I had been born rich . . .

IF I could meet "the right people" . . .

IF I had the talent that some people have . . .

IF I dared assert myself . . .

IF I only had embraced past opportunities . . .

IF people didn't get on my nerves . . .

IF I didn't have to keep house and look after the children . . .

IF I could save some money . . .

IF the boss only appreciated me . . .

IF I only had somebody to help me . . .

IF my family understood me . . .

IF I lived in a big city . . .

IF I could just get started . . .

IF I were only free . . .

IF I had the personality of some people . . .

IF I were not so fat . . .

IF my talents were known . . .

IF I could just get a "break" . . .

IF I could only get out of debt . . .

IF I hadn't failed . . .

IF I only knew how . . .

IF everybody didn't oppose me . . .

IF I didn't have so many worries . . .

IF I could marry the right person . . .

IF people weren't so dumb . . .

IF my family were not so extravagant . . .

IF I were sure of myself . . .

IF luck were not against me . . .

IF I had not been born under the wrong star . . .

IF it were not true that "what is to be will be" . . .

IF I did not have to work so hard . . .

IF I hadn't lost my money . . .

IF I lived in a different neighborhood . . .

IF I didn't have a "past" . . .

IF I only had a business of my own . . .

IF other people would only listen to me . . .

IF * * * and this is the greatest of them all * * *

I had the courage to see myself as I really am, I would *find out what is wrong with me, and correct it,* then I might have a chance to profit by my mistakes and learn something from the experience of others, for I know that there is something wrong with me, or I would now be where *I would have been if* I had spent more time analyzing my weaknesses, and less time building alibis to cover them.

Building alibis with which to explain away failure is a national pastime. The habit is as old as the human race, and *is fatal to success!* Why do people cling to their pet alibis? The answer is obvious. They defend their alibis because they create them! A man's alibi is the child of his own imagination. It is human nature to defend one's own brainchild.

Building alibis is a deeply rooted habit. Habits are difficult to break, especially when they provide justification for something we do. Plato had this truth in mind when he said, "The first and best victory is to conquer self. To be conquered by self is, of all things, the most shameful and vile."

Another philosopher had the same thought in mind when he said, "It was a great surprise to me when

I discovered that most of the ugliness I saw in others, was but a reflection of my own nature."

"It has always been a mystery to me," said Elbert Hubbard, "why people spend so much time deliberately fooling themselves by creating alibis to cover their weaknesses. If used differently, this same time would be sufficient to cure the weakness, then no alibis would be needed."

In parting, I would remind you that "Life is a checkerboard, and the player opposite you is time. If you hesitate before moving, or neglect to move promptly, your men will be wiped off the board by time. You are playing against a partner who will not tolerate indecision!"

Previously you may have had a logical excuse for not having forced Life to come through with whatever you asked, but that alibi is now obsolete, because you are in possession of the Master Key that unlocks the door to Life's bountiful riches.

The Master Key is intangible, but it is powerful! It is the privilege of creating, *in your own mind*, a burning desire for a definite form of riches. There is no penalty for the use of the Key, but there is a price you must pay if you do not use it. The price is failure. There is a reward of stupendous proportions if you put the Key to use. It is the satisfaction that comes to all who *conquer self and force Life to pay whatever is asked.*

The reward is worthy of your effort. Will you make the start and be convinced?

# SELF-CONTROL

You can never become a great leader nor a person of influence in the cause of justice until you have developed great self-control.

Before you can be of great service to your fellow men in any capacity you must master the common human tendency of anger, intolerance and cynicism.

When you permit another person to make you angry you are allowing that person to dominate you and drag you down to his level.

To develop self-control you must make liberal and systematic use of the Golden Rule philosophy; you must acquire the habit of forgiving those who annoy and arouse you to anger.

Intolerance and selfishness make very poor bedfellows for self-control. These qualities always clash when you try to house them together. One or the other must get out.

The first thing the shrewd lawyer usually does when he starts to cross-examine a witness is to make the witness angry and thereby cause him to lose his self-control.

Anger is a state of insanity!

The well-balanced person is a person who is slow at anger and who always remains cool and calculating in his procedure. He remains calm and deliberate under all conditions.

Such a person can succeed in all legitimate undertakings! To master conditions you must first master self! A person who exercises great self-control never slanders his neighbor. His tendency is to build up and not to tear down. Are you a person of self-control? If not, why do you not develop this great virtue?

# A DEFINITE AIM IN LIFE

Careful analysis of more than 10,000 people disclosed a remarkable weakness which 95 percent of them had in common—they had no definite aim in life!

Another notable fact disclosed by these ten thousand analyses was that those who were financially successful had a definite aim and a well formulated plan for achieving it.

As far as this writer has ever been able to ascertain, there are two steps which every successful person must take: first, he must formulate a very definite aim as an objective for which to strive, and secondly, he must reduce that aim to a concrete plan.

If you wish to witness a miracle which will equal anything that happened during biblical days, write out on paper a clear, concise statement of your aim in life, then memorize that which you have written.

Each night, just before you go to sleep; repeat your definite aim aloud several times, then, during the day, do everything within your power to further the achievement of that aim. In a short time the forces of the whole universe will seem to conspire to the end that you may realize your aim. Try it, doubting brother, try it.

## MORE ON A DEFINITE AIM FROM *THINK AND GROW RICH*

Every human being who reaches the age of understanding of the purpose of money wishes for it. *Wishing* will not bring riches. But *desiring* riches with a state of mind that becomes an obsession, then planning definite ways and means to acquire riches, and backing those plans with persistence which *does not recognize failure*, will bring riches.

The method by which desire for riches can be transmuted into its financial equivalent consists of six definite, practical steps, viz:

FIRST: **Fix in your mind the exact amount of money you desire.** It is not sufficient merely to say, "I want plenty of money." Be definite as to the amount. (There is a psychological reason for definiteness which will be described in a subsequent chapter.)

SECOND: **Determine exactly what you intend to give in return for the money you desire.** (There is no such reality as "something for nothing.")

THIRD: **Establish a definite date when you intend to** *possess* **the money you desire.**

FOURTH: **Create a definite plan for carrying out your desire,** and begin *at once,* whether you are ready or not, to put this plan into *action.*

FIFTH: **Write out a clear, concise statement** of the amount of money you intend to acquire, name the time limit for its acquisition, state what you intend to give in return for the money, and describe clearly the plan through which you intend to accumulate it.

SIXTH: **Read your written statement aloud, twice daily,** once just before retiring at night, and once after arising in the morning. As you read— see and feel and believe yourself already in possession of the money.

It is important that you follow the instructions described in these six steps. It is especially important that you observe and follow the instructions in the sixth paragraph. You may complain that it is impossible for you to "see yourself in possession of money" before you actually have it. Here is where a burning desire will come to your aid. If you truly desire money so keenly that your desire is an obsession, you will have no difficulty in convincing yourself that you will acquire it. The object is to want money, and to become so determined to have it that you convince yourself you will have it.

Only those who become "money conscious" ever accumulate great riches. "Money consciousness" means that the mind has become so thoroughly saturated with the desire for money, that one can see one's self already in possession of it.

# ENTHUSIASM & THE GOLDEN RULE

Excerpted from *The Law of Success*

## ENTHUSIASM

*"You Can Do It If You Believe You Can!"*

Enthusiasm is a state of mind that inspires and arouses one to put action into the task at hand. It does more than this—it is contagious, and vitally affects not only the enthusiast, but all with whom he comes in contact.

Enthusiasm bears the same relationship to a human being that steam does to the locomotive—it is the vital moving force that impels action. The greatest leaders of men are those who know how to inspire enthusiasm in their followers. Enthusiasm is the most important factor entering into salesmanship. It is, by far, the most vital factor that enters into public speaking. The finest sermon ever delivered would fall upon deaf ears if it were not backed with enthusiasm by the speaker.

## How Enthusiasm Will Affect You

Mix enthusiasm with your work and it will not seem hard or monotonous. Enthusiasm will so energize your entire body that you can get along with less than half the usual amount of sleep and at the same time it will enable you to perform from two to three times as much work as you usually perform in a given period, without fatigue.

For many years I have done most of my writing at night. One night, while I was enthusiastically at work over my typewriter, I looked out of the window of my study, just across the square from the Metropolitan tower, in New York City, and saw what seemed to be the most peculiar reflection of the moon on the tower. It was of a silvery gray shade, such as I had never seen before. Upon closer inspection I found that the reflection was that of the early morning sun and not that of the moon. It was daylight! I had been at work all night, but I was so engrossed in my work that the night had passed as though it were but an hour. I worked at my task all that day and all the following night without stopping, except for a small amount of light food.

Two nights and one day without sleep, and with but

little food, without the slightest evidence of fatigue, would not have been possible had I not kept my body energized with enthusiasm over the work at hand.

Enthusiasm is not merely a figure of speech; it is a vital force that you can harness and use with profit. Without it you would resemble an electric battery without electricity.

Enthusiasm is the vital force with which you recharge your body and develop a dynamic personality. Some people are blessed with natural enthusiasm, while others must acquire it. The procedure through which it may be developed is simple. It begins by the doing of the work or rendering of the service which one likes best. If you should be so situated that you cannot conveniently engage in the work which you like best, for the time being, then you can proceed along another line very effectively by adopting a definite chief aim that contemplates your engaging in that particular work at some future time.

Lack of capital and many other circumstances over which you have no immediate control may force you to engage in work which you do not like, but no one can stop you from determining in your own mind what your definite chief aim in life shall be, nor can anyone stop you from planning ways and means for translating this aim into reality, nor can anyone stop you from mixing enthusiasm with your plans.

Happiness, the final object of all human effort, is a state of mind that can be maintained only through the hope of future achievement. Happiness lies always in the future and never in the past. The happy person is the one who dreams of heights of achievement that are yet unattained. The home you intend to own, the money you intend to earn and place in the bank, the trip you intend to take when you can afford it, the position in life you intend to fill when you have prepared yourself, and the preparation, itself—these are the things that produce happiness. Likewise, these are the materials out of which your definite chief aim is formed; these are the things over which you may become enthusiastic, no matter what your present station in life may be.

More than twenty years ago I became enthusiastic over an idea. When the idea first took form in my mind I was unprepared to take even the first step toward its transformation into reality. But I nursed it in my mind—I became enthusiastic over it as I looked ahead, in my imagination, and saw the time when I would be prepared to make it a reality.

The idea was this: I wanted to become the editor of a magazine, based upon the Golden Rule, through which I could inspire people to keep up courage and deal with one another squarely.

Finally my chance came! and, on armistice day, 1918, I wrote the first editorial for what was to become the material realization of a hope that had lain dormant in my mind for nearly a score of years.

With enthusiasm I poured into that editorial the emotions which I had been developing in my heart over a period of more than twenty years. My dream had come true. My editorship of a national magazine had become a reality.

As I have stated, this editorial was written with enthusiasm. I took it to a man of my acquaintance and with enthusiasm I read it to him. The editorial ended in these words: "At last my twenty-year-old dream is about to come true. It takes money, and a lot of it, to publish a national magazine, and I haven't the slightest idea where I am going to get this essential factor, but this is worrying me not at all because I know I am going to get it somewhere!" As I wrote those lines, I mixed enthusiasm and faith with them.

I had hardly finished reading this editorial when the man to whom I read it—the first and only person to whom I had shown it—said:

"I can tell you where you are going to get the money, for I am going to supply it."

And he did!

Yes, enthusiasm is a vital force; so vital, in fact, that no man who has it highly developed can begin even to approximate his power of achievement.

I wish to repeat and to emphasize the fact that you may develop enthusiasm over your definite chief aim in life, no matter whether you are in position to achieve that purpose at this time or not. You may be a long way from realization of your definite chief aim, but if you will kindle the fire of enthusiasm in your heart, and keep it burning, before very long the obstacles that now stand in the way of your attainment of that purpose will melt away as if by the force of magic, and you will find yourself in possession of power that you did not know you possessed.

## How Your Enthusiasm Will Affect Others

We come, now, to the discussion of one of the most important subjects, namely, suggestion.

Suggestion is the principle through which your words and your acts and even your state of mind influence others. If you now understand and accept the principle of telepathy (the communication of thought from one mind to another without the aid of signs, symbols or sounds) as a reality, you of course understand why enthusiasm is contagious, and why it influences all within its radius.

When your own mind is vibrating at a high rate, because it has been stimulated with enthusiasm, that vibration registers in the minds of all within its radius, and especially in the minds of those with whom you come in close contact. When a public speaker "senses" the feeling that his audience is *"en rapport"* with him he merely recognizes the fact that his own enthusiasm has influenced the minds of his listeners until their minds are vibrating in harmony with his own.

When the salesman "senses" the fact that the "psychological" moment for closing a sale has arrived, he merely feels the effect of his own enthusiasm as it influences the mind of his prospective buyer and places that mind *"en rapport"* (in harmony) with his own.

The subject of suggestion constitutes so vitally an important part of this lesson, and of this entire course, that I will now proceed to describe the three mediums through which it usually operates; namely, what you say, what you do and what you think!

When you are enthusiastic over the goods you are selling or the services you are offering, or the speech you are delivering, your state of mind becomes obvious to all who hear you, by the tone of your voice. Whether you have ever thought of it in this way or not, it is the tone in which you make a statement, more than it is the statement itself, that carries conviction or fails to convince. No mere combination of words can ever take the place of a deep belief in a statement that is expressed with burning enthusiasm. Words are but devitalized sounds unless colored with feeling that is born of enthusiasm.

Here the printed word fails me, for I can never express with mere type and paper the difference between words that fall from unemotional lips, without the fire of enthusiasm back of them, and those which seem to pour forth from a heart that is bursting with eagerness for expression. The difference is there, however.

Thus, what you say, and the way in which you say it, conveys a meaning that may be just the opposite to what is intended. This accounts for many a failure by the salesman who presents his arguments in words which seem logical enough, but lack the coloring that can come only from enthusiasm that is born of sincerity and belief in the goods he is trying to sell. His words said one thing, but the tone of his voice suggested something entirely different; therefore, no sale was made.

That which you say is an important factor in the operation of the principle of suggestion, but not nearly so important as that which you do. Your acts will count for more than your words, and woe unto you if the two fail to harmonize.

Your thoughts constitute the most important of the three ways in which you apply the principle of suggestion, for the reason that they control the tone of your words and, to some extent at least, your actions. If your thoughts and your actions and your words harmonize, you are bound to influence those with whom you come in contact, more or less toward your way of thinking.

## The Golden Rule

Do unto others as you would have them do unto you!

We have heard that injunction expressed thousands of times, yet how many of us understand the law upon which it is based? To make this injunction somewhat clearer it might be well to state it more in detail, about as follows:

Do unto others as you would have them do unto you, bearing in mind the fact that human nature has a tendency to retaliate in kind.

Confucius must have had in mind the law of retaliation when he stated the Golden Rule philosophy in about this way:

Do not unto others that which you would not have them do unto you.

And he might well have added an explanation to the effect that the reason for his injunction was based upon the common tendency of man to retaliate in kind.

Those who do not understand the law upon which the Golden Rule is based are inclined to argue that it will not work, for the reason that men are inclined toward the principle of exacting "an eye for an eye and a tooth for a tooth," which is nothing more nor less than the law of retaliation. If they would go a step further in their reasoning they would understand that they are looking at the negative effects of this law, and that the selfsame law is capable of producing positive effects as well.

In other words, if you would not have your own eye plucked out, then insure against this misfortune by refraining from plucking out the other fellow's eye. Go a step further and render the other fellow an act of kindly, helpful service, and through the operation of this same law of retaliation he will render you a similar service.

And, if he should fail to reciprocate your kindness—what then?

You have profited, nevertheless, because of the effect of your act on your own sub-conscious mind!

Thus by indulging in acts of kindness and applying, always, the Golden Rule philosophy, you are sure of benefit from one source and at the same time you have a pretty fair chance of profiting from another source.

It might happen that you would base all of your acts toward others on the Golden Rule without enjoying any direct reciprocation for a long period of time, and it might so happen that those to whom you rendered those acts of kindness would never reciprocate, but meantime you have been adding vitality to your own character and sooner or later this positive character which you have been building will begin to assert itself and you will discover that you have been receiving compound interest on compound interest in return for those acts of kindness which appeared to have been wasted on those who neither appreciated nor reciprocated them.

Remember that your reputation is made by others, but your character is made by you!

You want your reputation to be a favorable one, but you cannot be sure that it will be for the reason that it is something that exists outside of your own control, in the minds of others. It is what others believe you to be. With your character it is different. Your character is that which you are, as the results of your thoughts and deeds. You control it. You can make it weak, good or bad. When you are satisfied and know in your mind that your character is above reproach you need not worry about your reputation, for it is as impossible for your character to be destroyed or damaged by anyone except yourself as it is to destroy matter or energy.

It was this truth that Emerson had in mind when he said: "A political victory, a rise of rents, the recovery of your sick or the return of your absent friend, or some other quite external event raises your spirits, and you think your days are prepared for you. Do not believe it. It can never be so. Nothing can bring you peace but yourself. Nothing can bring you peace but the triumph of principles."

One reason for being just toward others is the fact that such action may cause them to reciprocate, in kind, but a better reason is the fact that kindness and justice toward others develop positive character in all who indulge in these acts.

You may withhold from me the reward to which I am entitled for rendering you helpful service, but no one can deprive me of the benefit I will derive from the rendering of that service in so far as it adds to my own character.

# ABOUT THE AUTHOR

**NAPOLEON HILL** was born in 1883 in a one-room cabin on the Pound River in Wise County, Virginia. He is the author of the motivational classics *The Laws of Success* and *Think and Grow Rich*. Hill passed away in November 1970 after a long and successful career writing, teaching, and lecturing about the principles of success. His lifework continues under the direction of The Napoleon Hill Foundation.